A Life Worth Living

JOSEPH PRINCE

A Life Worth Living

ISBN 981-05-3728-X
© Copyright Joseph Prince, 2006

Joseph Prince Resources
www.JosephPrince.com

Printed in the Republic of Singapore
First edition, seventeenth print: March 2016

contents

Prepare For Increased Blessing

One Saturday night in early 2004, I woke up with a sense that God wanted to talk to me. "Lord, speak to me," I responded. I began to speak in tongues for a while and then I interpreted the tongues. I heard the Lord say to me, "The year 2004 will be a year of more, a thousand times more, in every area of your life."

The Lord instructed me to prepare our church to receive His thousand-fold blessing. The result has been amazing and I give God all the glory for it. My church has seen miraculous increase in many areas. We began hearing testimonies from people who were experiencing supernatural debt cancellations, from people who had been blessed with new homes and from people who were given much better salaries when they got new jobs. And there were physical miracles as well, including the healing of complete deafness in one ear and the healing of a spinal injury caused by a car accident. In fact, there are just too many to list here.

The message in this book is what the Lord told me to teach my church. Today, I believe this message is for the whole church, the body of Christ. It's not just a message for my church.

What I'm going to share with you is directly from the Lord, so it's a fresh message, like the smell of freshly baked bread, like the smell of fresh rain. And like bread and rain, it will satisfy your hunger and quench your thirst.

By the way, I believe that when God promised our church one thousand times more, He did not mean one thousand more wives! When it comes to people, it's quality, not necessarily quantity that counts. So God wants to **bless** you a thousand times more. He wants to bless your family, your business, your career, your relationships, your health and your church. He wants to enhance your life one thousand times more. He wants you to be plentiful and abundant. Only He can give you a life that is worth living!

All those who accept and believe this message will be ushered effortlessly into one-thousand-times-more blessing, into divine provision with a purpose. And it won't happen by might nor by power, but by God's Spirit alone.

Are you ready for more, even a thousand times more? If so, God wants you to seek first His kingdom and His righteousness, and all these blessings shall be added unto you. But don't mix up His righteousness with your own righteousness. He wants you to seek **His** righteousness — He wants you to walk in the gift of righteousness that Jesus died to purchase for you. Romans 5:17 says that *"those who receive abundance of grace and of the gift of righteousness will reign in life through the One, Jesus Christ"*.

God wants you to seek His kingdom and His righteousness because a life in which you are on the throne is truly a miserable life! God loves you too much to let you live like that. He knows that only with Jesus in the centre of your life will you be fulfilled and safe. God wants us to stop focusing on ourselves and to start concentrating on Jesus. When we seek first His kingdom and His righteousness, God says in Matthew 6:33 that *"all these things shall be added to you"*. In other words, seek first His kingdom and His righteousness, and God promises that He will take care of the rest. Then, we will experience a fulfilled life.

That, my friend, is a life worth living!

chapter

1

Forget The Fantasies

chapter 1

Forget The Fantasies

Learn From The Mistakes The Bible Characters Made

In my role as a pastor, I have met so many people who share with me their pain and hardships. Too many lives have been riddled with trouble, mostly self-inflicted. I have counselled so many people during my two decades in the ministry. Some choose to follow my advice, others don't.

The Bible is full of truths showing us how to live rewarding and abundant lives. Yet, so many people choose not to follow biblical blueprints for their lives. Instead, they choose to follow their fantasies and pleasures. They give in to the temptations of fame and fortune that this world promises through movies, magazines and television programmes. I've yet to see one person, who after indulging in the pleasures of this world, return to me to say that it was worth it. Quite the opposite — they return and tell me that their lives are empty, that they hate life. I've met more than one who has confessed to me that they are suicidal. For them, life is not worth living.

While many choose not to, we can all learn from the mistakes of others. The Bible is one book that can teach us how to live a life worth living. Reading the Bible, you'll learn from the sufferings of David, Solomon, Samson, Jacob, Lot, Samuel and many others. But there are many people who choose not to learn from the sufferings of others. Even after reading about how David and Solomon made their mistakes and suffered the consequences, they are still prepared to make the same mistakes themselves.

Two to three years down the road, after thinking that they have progressed, they find themselves back at square one. It's like playing the game Snakes and Ladders. You climb the ladders a few times over the years, but then you land on the snake's head and slide back down again!

Have You Ever Fantasised About Having More Money And Influence?

Have you ever fantasised about money? Have you ever thought to yourself, "If I had enough money to buy whatever I want, to travel wherever I want, to marry whoever I want... "? Have you ever wondered what it would be like to be born in a very rich family, to have lots of influence and power?

One day, when I was very tired, I asked my wife to massage my head and shoulders. She was wonderful. Her hands soothed my sore muscles and I began to relax. But after a short while, she grew tired and stopped. I began to fantasise: What if I was a king? I'd have lots of servants, and they would massage my head and shoulders because if they didn't, they'd soon have no hands to massage anyone! Have you, like me, ever thought what it would be like to have a massage that goes on forever?

Have you ever thought to yourself, "What if I could have whatever my eyes see and like"? Would that be a life worth living? There is a man in the Bible who lived a life that many men and women would fantasise about. In the book of Ecclesiastes, we see that King Solomon indulged in everything and anything his flesh desired.

Solomon said in Ecclesiastes 2:1–11:

> [1]I said in my heart, "Come now, I will test you with mirth; therefore enjoy pleasure"; but surely, this also was vanity. [2]I said of laughter — "Madness!"; and of mirth, "What does it accomplish?" [3]I searched in my heart how to gratify my flesh with wine, while guiding my heart with wisdom, and how to lay hold on folly, till I might see what was good for the sons of men to do under heaven all the days of their lives.
>
> [4]I made my works great, I built myself houses, and planted myself vineyards. [5]I

made myself gardens and orchards, and I planted all kinds of fruit trees in them. [6]I made myself water pools from which to water the growing trees of the grove. [7]I acquired male and female servants, and had servants born in my house. Yes, I had greater possessions of herds and flocks than all who were in Jerusalem before me. [8]I also gathered for myself silver and gold and the special treasures of kings and of the provinces. I acquired male and female singers, the delights of the sons of men, and musical instruments of all kinds.

[9]So I became great and excelled more than all who were before me in Jerusalem. Also my wisdom remained with me. [10]Whatever my eyes desired I did not keep from them. I did not withhold my heart from any pleasure, for my heart rejoiced in all my labour; and this was my reward from all my labour. [11]Then I looked on all the works that my hands had done and on the labour in which I had toiled; and indeed all was vanity and grasping for the wind. There was no profit under the sun.

Solomon Indulged In Every Fantasy

I'm sure that many of us have had similar fantasies. Men who love building can relate to this: "If I had no money restrictions, and I had all the power and means to build and design houses the way I like…" Solomon was the original Bob the Builder! Could he do it? Yes, he could because he had the money!

Solomon built God a temple. Then, the temple was the most expensive building in the world. After that, he built his own house, his palace. Do you know how long he took to build his palace? Seven years! To women, that may be a nightmare! To men who love building, that is a fantasy. Whatever you may fantasise about, this man did! Solomon indulged in every fantasy. He also grew fruit trees and built water pools. He was a great horticulturalist.

Notice that Solomon says in verse 7, "I acquired male and female servants". So he could enjoy a massage any time he wanted! And in the original Hebrew, *"musical instruments of all kinds"* (verse 8) translates to "concubines of all kinds". Solomon had concubines of all kinds. The Bible tells us that Solomon had 300 concubines and 700 wives. Solomon was a man who had everything. If there was a downside to all this, it would be that he also had 700 mothers-in-law!

Don't forget that God gave him wisdom, favour, influence and power to get wealth, but God didn't give him the results or outcomes of his wealth. God didn't give him the results or outcomes of his influence. God didn't give him the results or outcomes of his wisdom and favour. Nonetheless, Solomon's wisdom and favour came from God.

Verse 9 says:

> **⁹So I became great and excelled more than all who were before me in Jerusalem…**

Solomon became great and whatever he saw and liked, he took. What would men and women give for that! Would you call that a life worth living?

Let's see how Solomon's life of fantasy unravels (verses 10–11):

> **¹⁰Whatever my eyes desired I did not keep from them. I did not withhold my heart from any pleasure, for my heart rejoiced in**

all my labour; and this was my reward from all my labour. [11]Then I looked on all the works that my hands had done and on the labour in which I had toiled; and indeed all was vanity and grasping for the wind. There was no profit under the sun.

The book of Ecclesiastes is a story of a backslidden man. Solomon was a man who once knew God, but later, even though he still had his God-given gifts, he turned his heart away from God. Here is a man who did everything under the sun and yet despaired of life.

> If you only experience things under the sun, you'll always be unfulfilled.

The lesson here is that whenever your thoughts become earthly and focus on things under the sun, you despair. We must never forget that God is above the sun. When he wrote the book of Proverbs and Song of Solomon, Solomon's thoughts were heavenly and he spoke about things above the sun. But in Ecclesiastes, we see that he was focused on things below the sun and his life had no more meaning.

If You Live Life 'Under The Sun', You'll Despair

Solomon, the man who experienced everything, leaves us a clue in a phrase that appears throughout the book of Ecclesiastes — *"under the sun"*. Solomon lived life enjoying all earthly pleasures. Indeed, he lived life indulging in everything under the sun. And yet, he grew very depressed (verse 11):

> [11]Then I looked on all the works that my hands had done and on the labour in which I had toiled; and indeed all was vanity and grasping for the wind. There was no profit under the sun.

My friend, if you only experience things under the sun, deep down, you'll always be unfulfilled, you'll always be empty on the inside.

When I was in National Service, I was assigned to the Singapore navy. I remember that over a period of a month, our ship sailed to a number of destinations. One day, we docked in Taiwan and we all took some R&R leave. That meant that we were supposed to go out and enjoy ourselves. I went along with my friends to a restaurant and we had a good time. When we finished our meal, my friends decided that they wanted to go "floor dancing". Now, I was already a practising Christian and I remember thinking to myself, "How can the floor dance?"

I decided not to follow them and before they set off, I said to them, "Look, whatever you guys want to do, just go ahead, but I'm going back to the ship." So I returned to the ship. The few sailors who were on duty back on the ship were cursing having to do duty that night. When they saw me return early from R&R, they thought that I was sick. Later, when they knew the reason for my coming back early, they made fun of me and said, "You Christian! The night is young! Why don't you drink and be happy!" I went to my room, read some books and spent time with Jesus on my bunk.

Some of you might say, "Pastor Prince, you missed out on a good night!" Perhaps I did, but wait and see what happened next. The men all returned to the ship after their R&R. Then, on the journey back to Singapore, one by one my friends came to me and said, "I don't know what happened that night, but can you help me? I think I might have caught a disease! When I urinate, it hurts! I might have Aids! It was my first time being unfaithful. I have a wife and kids back home. I don't know why I did it."

What a horrible thought! A possible death sentence for one moment of gratification! Strange, isn't it? One moment, these men are shouting, "The night is young, drink and be merry!" The next moment, they are facing a possible lethal disease. Now, I ask you: Who was the merry one on that return trip to Singapore?

By the way, one of those men did contract a venereal disease, but after I prayed for him, the Lord healed him and he later gave his life to Jesus.

Living On 'That Side Of The Night'

I'm a truly blessed man. From a young age, God taught me to live a life worth living. And it wasn't just through His Word and counselling that I saw how sad it is to live for just one moment of gratification. He even gave me a dream to teach me this.

Some years ago, I had a dream and I woke up knowing that God had spoken to me in that dream. I knew that the dream was from God because when God gives you a dream, it has His fingerprints all over it. I do not know how, but in my dream, I ended up contracting Aids! I don't even remember having sex. But for some reason, He gave me a dream in which I just knew that I had been unfaithful to my wife and I had committed a sin.

It was so real. I woke up remembering that I had sinned in that dream. In my dream, I actually lived my life day after day, aware of my sin and my disease. In my dream, I looked at my beautiful, loving wife and thought to myself, "How stupid can you be!" But I could not turn back the clock. The act had been committed. I looked at my daughter and thought to myself, "I may not live to see her grow up." I looked at my church and said, "I have to resign." All from just one moment of gratification!

I said to God, "I'm so sorry! If only I can turn back the clock!" Then, I woke up. That dream was so real that even when I woke up, I thought that I was still dreaming. I thought that my real life was a dream and that my dream was real life. When I realised that it was all a dream, I almost shouted, "It was a dream! Praise God, it was a dream! Thank you, Lord Jesus!"

Then, I asked, "Lord, why did you give me that dream?" And the Lord said to me, "I gave you the

> Dead fish float downstream, but live fish can swim upstream!

dream so that you'll understand how people feel after they have sinned. There are many men who live on this side of the night and I wanted you to experience this side of the night in a dream so that you could see firsthand what people are going through." After the dream, I felt grateful for living a life worth living, a life that's "above the sun".

We Are Meant To Live Lives 'Above The Sun'

All of us are meant to live lives above the sun. For me, life is full, not empty. To me, life is not grasping for the wind. I don't know about you, but I'm enjoying life! I enjoy my family, I enjoy my wife, I enjoy my daughter, I enjoy my job, I enjoy my church... I enjoy my life! Jesus said in John 10:10, *"I have come that they may have life, and that they may have it more abundantly."* That is a life worth living!

Your heart may be beating normally, but that does not mean that you are alive. You may be healthy physically, but you may be dead spiritually, like a walking zombie! Dead fish float downstream, but live fish can swim upstream! God wants to give you life to swim upstream, not to flow with the current. You are meant to have life more abundantly. But when a man has forgotten God and his thoughts are only of things under the sun, and he does everything he wants to gratify his flesh, in the end, like Solomon, he'll say, "All was vanity and grasping for the wind!" (Ecclesiastes 2:11) I tell you, a man who does not withhold from his eyes whatever his heart desires, in the end, he'll say, "All was vanity and grasping for the wind!"

The devil will try to put fantasies in your mind. He'll try saying to you, "You're missing out on life if you don't try everything under the sun." A rich playboy in the United States woke up one morning beside the latest girl in his bed, looked in the mirror and admitted, "I'm a lonely man!"

We have all heard of people who were rich and famous, who were successful in their fields of endeavour, who were good-looking, and yet in the end, they despaired of life. Elizabeth Taylor was once quoted in a fashionable newspaper as saying, "God knows I have tried. I have tried fame, food, men, drugs and drink, but I have never found peace." The article described how she looked at her sleeping mother so very near death and said sadly, "Maybe death is the only peace."

Just six weeks before he died, Elvis Presley was asked by a reporter, "Elvis, when you started playing music, you said that you wanted three things in life. You wanted to be rich, you wanted to be famous and you wanted to be happy. Are you happy, Elvis?" Elvis replied, "No, I am as lonely as hell."

For people like these, life held no more meaning. For them, life was empty. For them, life was not worth living.

Divine Provision With A Purpose

chapter 2

Divine Provision With A Purpose

The Love Of Money Can Easily Ensnare Us

A life worth living is a life in which we experience God's abundant provision for a divine purpose. However, to many Christians, the idea of prosperity seems dangerous because it has the potential to take us away from our purpose. And there is good reason to be cautious because the love of money can so easily ensnare us.

Jesus told the parable of the rich fool in Luke 12:13–21:

>[13]Then one from the crowd said to Him, "Teacher, tell my brother to divide the inheritance with me." [14]But He said to him, "Man, who made Me a judge or an arbitrator over you?" [15]And He said to them, "Take heed and beware of covetousness, for one's life does not consist in the abundance of the things he possesses."
>
>[16]Then He spoke a parable to them, saying: "The ground of a certain rich man yielded plentifully. [17]And he thought within himself, saying, 'What shall I do, since I have no room to store my crops?' [18]So he said, 'I will do this: I will pull down my barns and build greater, and there I will store all my crops and my goods. [19]And I will say to my soul, 'Soul, you have many goods laid up for many years; take your ease; eat, drink, and be merry.'" [20]But God said to him, 'Fool! This night your soul will be required of you; then whose will those

things be which you have provided?'

²¹"So is he who lays up treasure for himself, and is not rich toward God."

Beware of covetousness, Jesus says in verse 15. To covet is to yearn for and to crave something that is not yours. The world and its media fight for your attention to entice you to want more than you have, to buy things you don't need, with money you don't have, to impress people who don't care!

An Abundance Of Material Things Will Not Determine Quality Of Life

Now, God is not against you having an abundance of things. That's not what Jesus is saying here in this passage of scripture. He is against things having you, not you having things. In fact, Jesus says in Luke 12:30 that our heavenly Father knows that we have need of material things. Matthew 6:33 tells us:

³³But seek first the kingdom of God and

His righteousness, and all these things [including material things] shall be added to you.

So God is not against us having material possessions, but it's wrong to think that an abundance of possessions will determine the quality of our lives. Jesus Himself said in Luke 12:15 that a man's life *"does not consist in the abundance of things he possesses"*.

God not only wants you to have a thousand times more, He also wants you to have quality of life — a life worth living. Even though God wants you to have an abundance of things, a life worth living is made up not only of an abundance of things.

The Blessing Of The Lord Brings Fruitfulness

In Luke 12:16, Jesus began to share the parable of the rich fool with the crowd:

> [16]Then He spoke a parable to them, saying: "The ground of a certain rich man yielded plentifully.

Let's ponder that. Whenever you find that the ground — or your career or your relationships — is yielding plentifully, what is that a sign of? It's a sign of God's blessing. It's obvious that God blessed this rich man in the parable. His ground was very fruitful.

But he did not know that it was the blessing of God. When your career is blessed, who is blessing you? When your marriage is blessed, who is blessing you? When your business is blessed, who is blessing you? The Lord is blessing you! The same scripture goes on to say in verse 17:

> [17]And he thought within himself, saying, 'What shall I do, since I have no room to store my crops?'

Notice the word "I" used here? If you count the number of times the personal pronoun "I" is used in the three verses from 17 to 19, you'll find that the rich fool used the word "I" six times.

Let's read the passage again:

> [17]And he thought within himself, saying, 'What shall I do, since I have no room to

store my crops?' ¹⁸So he said, 'I will do this: I will pull down my barns and build greater, and there I will store all my crops and my goods. ¹⁹And I will say to my soul, 'Soul, you have many goods laid up for many years; take your ease; eat, drink, and be merry." ²⁰But God said to him, 'Fool! This night your soul will be required of you; then whose will those things be which you have provided?'

²¹"So is he who lays up treasure for himself, and is not rich toward God."

This shows his preoccupation with self and earthly pursuits. Why? Because in the Bible, "6" is the number of man and man is earthly. So this man was chasing only earthly things to be rich for himself.

God Wants You To Be Rich Towards Him

I've said before that God is not against you having things, but God wants you to be rich towards **Him**. It's divine provision with a purpose. Believe that this year, you will experience not just a thousand times more, but you will be a thousand times more rich towards God. All of a sudden, there'll be things in your life you've never had before. You'll travel to places you never expected to go. It may be for a holiday or for work or for ministry… it may be all three! But let us not forget that as we see abundant increase in our lives, the purpose is to be rich towards God.

> The love of money is the root of all evil, not money itself.

If the quality of a man's life depends on how much he has, then the lives of the rich and famous — from movie stars to pop stars to sports stars — would be examples to us on how we too should live. But how many of them are truly happy? How many of them lead comfortable and balanced lives? How many of them stay married to one wife for more than 10 years? There are people with lots of money who don't seem to be enjoying life, who seem to be searching for love in all the wrong places.

Rich And Poor Have Problems With Money

People think that only the rich have problems with money. That's just not true. We must eradicate this myth. Perpetrators of this myth tell us, "Be careful about becoming rich or you'll end up with money problems, marriage problems and health problems." "It's just not worth it!" they say.

Let me tell you that there are people who are poor who covet money. The Bible does not say, "Money is the root of all evil." 1 Timothy 6:10 has been misquoted too many times. This scripture says that the *love of money* is the root of all evil, not money itself. There are poor people who think of money all day long. They sit at home and worry about money all day. They are full of anxiety about money. When they wake up in the morning, the first thing on their mind is, "We have no money... we need to get more money!" They don't work for fulfilment or for the glory of God, they work to get money to buy food and clothing. Even when they don't have money, they worry about money. That is the **love** of money.

You don't have to be rich to have the love of money. If it's riches that make people love money, then Abraham, Joseph and David would have loved money. The Bible tells us that these men were rich, but they loved God, not money. There are many people like Abraham, Joseph and David who love God, and who use their money to worship Him.

> A poor man steals one watermelon, a rich man steals a whole truck of watermelons!

However, there are people who when their level of wealth increases, divorce their wives and stop attending church. There are also people who are busy finding their way to Viva Las Vegas! They are focused on getting rich quickly. Research has shown that people who obtain quick money, such as winning a lucky draw or lottery, also lose it quickly. Some people might say, "Aha! See that proves that money destroys people." Well, no, the Bible says in Proverbs 1:32 (KJV) that prosperity destroys **fools**.

Good People Use Money For Good Purposes

On the other hand, there are people who, when they experience a sudden blessing, use the blessing to sponsor more missionaries around the world. They use their wealth to sponsor gospel rallies. They use it to bless orphanages. They use it to bless the work of God. A good man will see money on the floor, pick it up and give it to a good cause. The money then becomes good money. But if an evil man picks it up, it becomes evil money.

Of course, there are always rich people who are covetous as well. There are rich people who are small-hearted and selfish. One difference between a poor man and a rich man is this: A poor man steals one watermelon, a rich man steals a whole truck of watermelons! You see, the capacity for good and evil increases with an increase in wealth. So it is really about what is in your heart.

Money reveals what's in your heart. If you are a good person, an increase in your wealth will reveal the good that's in your heart. If you are a bad person, more money will reveal the evil that has been in your heart all along. Some people don't commit adultery simply because they don't have the money to do it, but their heart is focused on it. The moment they acquire money, they divorce their wives. Their wives don't see them any more and their children don't see them any more.

Some Need Preparation Before Financial Increase

It's not that God doesn't want to bring money into some people's lives. God sees that the characters of some people need adjustment before they can be entrusted with more wealth. Their hearts need more grace from God so that the fruits of the Spirit — love, joy, peace, longsuffering, kindness, goodness, faithfulness, gentleness and self-control (Galatians 5:22–23) — can be made manifest in their lives. Only then will they be ready for God's increase — even a thousand-fold increase.

God wants to give you a thousand times more, but He loves you too much to let the thousand times more destroy you. God loves you too much to let the thousand times more blessing move you out of the position of favour, the place of great blessing. If you open your heart to the grace of God and you're a man or woman of integrity, when God blesses you with much, you will think of other people you can bless. My friend, it all comes back to the heart.

Let's look at the rich man in Luke 12 again:

> [16]Then He spoke a parable to them, saying: "The ground of a certain rich man yielded plentifully. [17]And he thought within himself, saying, 'What shall I do, since I have no room to store my crops?'

This man's heart was selfish. When his ground brought forth plentifully, he started thinking of himself. He began to talk to himself, saying, "What shall I do? I have no more room. Okay, this is what I'll do: I'll build bigger barns. I'll build bigger storehouses and I'll... " His response to wealth was "I... I... I..."

Whatever the amount of money that comes into your life, tithe. Because what you tithe on becomes holy and what is holy is powerful.

Tithe The 10 Per Cent And Sanctify The 90 Per Cent

Tithing is a simple act of faith in God and His promises. Abraham is a great example of a man of real faith. In Genesis 14, we find that after his victory over four kings, Abraham met Melchizedek, king of Salem (who is also a picture of our Lord Jesus Christ).

Verse 20 says:

> [20]And blessed be God Most High, who has delivered your enemies into your hand." And he gave him a tithe of all.

Abraham was the first person to tithe to the Lord and we know that God blessed Abraham with riches.

In Romans 11:16, Paul says:

> [16]For if the firstfruit is holy, the lump is also holy; and if the root is holy, so are the branches.

If the firstfruit is holy, the lump is also holy.

When you give one-tenth of what you have to God, it is holy to the Lord. (Leviticus 27:30) The word "tithe" in Hebrew literally means "one-tenth". And when the first 10 per cent — or firstfruit — is holy, the rest is holy. It becomes sanctified. And what the Lord sanctifies, the devil cannot touch!

Malachi 3:10 says:

> [10]Bring all the tithes into the storehouse, that there may be food in My house, and try Me now in this," says the Lord of hosts, "If I will not open for you the windows of heaven and pour out for you such blessing that there will not be room enough to receive it.

Why does God ask you to tithe on your salary? Not for **His** sake, but for **your** sake. Generally speaking, in the world, money is actually abused. More and more evil people are using money for more evil purposes. But as a child of God, when you receive money, you tithe. Why? Because Romans 11:16 tells us that if the firstfruit is holy, the rest is holy. If the 10 per cent is holy, the 90 per cent will also be sanctified. You may ask, "But, Pastor Prince, why do I want my salary to be sanctified?" One simple reason is this: The devil cannot touch what is holy. The devil can only touch what is dirty or unsanctified.

It is not an unreasonable request that God makes of you. God does not ask for 100 per cent of your salary. He's the only senior partner who owns everything and sponsors everything, and yet, asks from you, the junior partner, His share of only 10 per cent! Even then, the junior partner often continues to negotiate with the senior partner. There is no condemnation in that, but it means that you miss out on the rewards.

God doesn't fall off his throne just because you forgot to tithe. But if you don't tithe, you are just not positioning yourself for greater blessings from God. God wants to bless you because He loves you. And if you are able to tithe, it also means that you are able to keep money as a servant and God as your God, rather than the other way around.

Don't Wait For Your Ship To Come In Before You Start Tithing

There will always be someone who says, "Pastor Prince, when my ship comes in, I'll build God a church!" I have had people say to me down through the years, "When my ship comes in... When I win the lottery... When I win my lucky draw... I'll tithe and I'll build God the biggest church in Singapore!" Forget those promises. The test is this: Now, when your small boat comes in, when your sampan comes in, tithe on that. Don't wait for the big one. If you cannot tithe on what you have now, forget about tithing when your ship comes in!

> Faithful tithing keeps you safe and positions you for greater blessings from God.

There is a lady who attends my church whom the Lord blessed with more than a million dollars within one day. She had been tithing faithfully for nearly a year before she received the million dollars. She tithed on whatever income she received. She was tithing regularly. Then, when the Lord blessed her, the first thing she did was she tithed on the million dollars. Do you know why it wasn't too hard for her? She had been faithfully tithing before the increased blessing. So forget about waiting for the ship to come in before you tithe. Let's focus now on the little boats, the sampans, and tithe on these.

Faithful tithing keeps you safe and positions you for greater blessings from God. And it prepares you for the thousand-fold blessing that God wants to give you.

3

A Christ-Centred Life

chapter 3

A Christ-Centred Life

Law Is You Working, Grace Is God Working

A life worth living is a life lived under the grace of God. What a wonderful place to be! But people always ask me, "Pastor Prince, how do I know if I am living under grace or under law?" You are under law whenever you find yourself saying, "Am I pleasing to God? Am I doing all right? Because I did something wrong, I wonder if God is displeased with me?"

Whenever you are conscious of what you are to God, you are living under law. Law is what you are to be before God. Grace is what God is to you. Whenever you are conscious of what God is to you, you are under grace.

Law says, "**I** am working." Grace says, "**God** is working." Law is when I work. Grace is when God works. Right now, even as I am conveying this message to you, there's an inward rest in me. I'm conveying a message, but I'm not working because it's Christ in me who is working. I cease my work and I look to Him. I'm under grace, not under law. Under law, I have to work while God rests. Under grace, God works and I rest. All good things and blessings are accomplished when **God** works. When **I** work, the result is bad, very bad. When God works, the result can be nothing but perfect!

> God is working in you right now as you read this book.

Choose Grace Over Law

It's time for us to realise that we're no longer under law. Law is the consciousness of self and how short we fall of God's glory. Law focuses on what we are supposed to be before God and what we are not supposed to be before God.

How conscious are you of your faults and failures? God wants you to stop focusing on them. Focus on Him instead. Even as you are now seated reading this book, do you know that God is working in your life? Do you know right now that God is working in your body, in your mind and in your heart? Do you really know that? God is working in you right now as you read this book.

You may ask, "How can God be working when I am sitting still?" God works all the more in us when we sit still and let God be God. And when God works, His results are perfect.

So when you believe that God is working, it's not a matter of sitting down and doing nothing. You must believe that God is working. You must believe that right now, God is working in your life. You must believe that right now,

God is working on your health. Right now, God is working in your family. That's God's grace and the only response required of us is that we believe. The most pleasing thing you can do before God is to believe Him, to trust Him.

So what is grace? Grace is to forget about self and to be Christ-occupied. When He becomes the central figure in your life, your life will be filled with purpose and meaning. Jesus said in John 10:10:

> [10]The thief does not come except to steal, and to kill, and to destroy. I have come that they may have life, and that they may have it more abundantly.

If You Want To See What God Is Like, Look At Jesus

How do you become more Christ-centred? By discovering more of who He is. My Bible tells me in Colossians 1:15 that Jesus is the image of the invisible God. My friend, if you want to see what God is like, look at Jesus. Throughout the books of Matthew, Mark, Luke and John, He had compassion on the needy, He cleansed the lepers, He opened blind eyes and restored deaf ears, He raised the dead and He loved little children.

The one who created everything walked on this earth with us. He showed us what God is like because He is the image of the invisible God. John 1:3 says, *"All things were made through Him, and without Him nothing was made that was made."*

Everything that you see in creation was created by our Lord Jesus Christ. The Bible says in Colossians 1:16 that all things *"visible and invisible"* — whether thrones, dominions, principalities or powers — were made by Him. He created the stars, the sun and the moon. Whether you can see it or you can't see it, He made it.

It's beautiful sometimes to see Jesus in "lowly grace". God is not showy and pretentious like man. We try to get a bit of a name for ourselves. We tend to crave attention. God may have created a particular type of fish to demonstrate one of man's weaknesses. It's known as the pufferfish. When threatened, it inflates itself by swallowing water. It puffs itself up to make it look bigger than it really is.

But Jesus is not like that. When He chose the place in which He was to be born, He didn't choose a palace, but a smelly cave. The King of all kings was to be born in a lowly manger. He walked among fishermen, not royalty. He chose fishermen and tax collectors as His disciples. This is what we call "lowly grace". It's a beautiful picture.

But don't forget that the hands that held and blessed children also created the stars, the moon and the millions of suns beyond our sun. And when those same hands were nailed to the cross, it is no wonder there were three hours of darkness in the middle of that day.

Your Purpose In Life — Do Whatever You Do For God's Glory

Do you want purpose in your life? The Bible tells us in Colossians 1:16 that Jesus is the creator of all things for a reason — *"All things were created through Him and for Him"*. We find here that there

is a purpose to life. You can have purpose in your marriage. When you get married, don't marry for one another, marry and love one another for Him. Build purpose into your children. Nurture your children for Him and for His glory. Have purpose in your career. Develop your career for Him.

If you are working for any other reason, your life won't have purpose. You might say, "I'm working for my family to put food on the table." My friend, that's just an existence, not a purpose. Do everything for the Lord Jesus and you will experience life more abundantly. Your life will be worth living. If you are serving your church or the community in some way — even if you are picking up litter — do it all for His glory. When your life takes on purpose beyond yourself, life takes on meaning beyond mere existence. The smallest task and the lowest paid job are no longer boring.

In everything you do, do it for His glory. When I preach, I don't preach for man's favour, I preach for His glory. In everything, even when you eat and drink, do it for His glory because all things were made through Him and for Him.

When people say and write bad things about me, I have a clear conscience because I know that whatever I do, I do for His glory, not for man. My friend, that is a life worth living.

When He Is Glorified, Everybody Is Edified

Do everything to glorify God and you will find that you no longer have to look over your shoulder to see what people are saying about you. Man's opinions will no longer be important. When He is glorified, everybody is edified. The sick are healed, the blind see and the dead are raised. Whenever He is glorified, everything in the universe is at peace. If I live for my glory and for my fame, then I am empty. At the end of it all, like Solomon, I will hate life.

> When you live for His glory, there will be deep fulfilment in everything you do.

You will lead a shallow life if all you seek is people's approval. In contrast, God's affirmation is deep and fulfilling. When you live life for His glory, no one may know what you do, no one may see what you do and no one may compliment you for what you do. But when you live for His glory, there will be deep fulfilment in everything you do. When you sleep at night, your sleep will be peaceful and refreshing.

When you do everything to glorify Him, people **will** begin to notice. We want our lives to be blessed so that when people look at us, they'll say that the God we serve must truly be God. Why do you want to be blessed this year? Why do you want a thousand times more this year? For self-gratification? No, for Him and for His glory. When God blesses us, we have opportunity to tell our friends about God. Your career, your health, your marriage and your business are blessed not for your enjoyment only, but also for a higher reason — for His glory.

Christ Holds Everything Together

Colossians 1:17 says, *"And He is before all things, and in Him all things consist."* The Greek word for "consist" means "held together". Scientists today tell us that every matter is made of atoms. Now, scientists will also tell us that atoms are made up of electrons, protons and neutrons. But did you know that while scientists can tell us that everything in our world can be broken down into a tiny unit called an atom, they cannot tell us what holds the atom together? They just don't know what force holds the atom together! My Bible tells me in Colossians 1:17 that by Christ, all things are held together. That's why when Christ comes into your life, you are held together. You become integrated into His life.

> Just attending a marriage seminar will not hold your marriage together.

But those who are without Christ and those who are "carnal" Christians have their lives torn in many directions. While their mind is going in one direction, their mouth is going in another direction, their heart is going in a third direction and their feet are going in a completely different direction altogether. Their lives are like a long internal civil war. They are not held together, they are not integrated and that's why they have no integrity. For them, life is not fulfilling, life is not worth living. When Christ comes into your life, He integrates you and He brings peace to the warring factions of your life. After all, He is called the Prince of Peace. (Isaiah 9:6)

A Marriage Is Only Blessed With Christ In The Centre

A blessed marriage is one in which Christ is in the centre. Everything in that marriage revolves around Christ. Only then will all things be held together in that marriage. You cannot build a marriage on human love. The Bible says in Ephesians 5:25, *"Husbands, love your wives, just as Christ also loved the church and gave Himself for her."* The type of "love" here is *agape* love, which means the love of Christ. So those of us who are married are to love our wives or husbands with the love of Jesus Himself.

Just attending a marriage seminar will not hold your marriage together. That is a humanistic solution. The wisdom of the world tells you that husbands must do this, this and this, and wives must do that, that and that, then everything will be okay. Well-qualified psychologists will tell you that you are to do this and this in the bedroom, and read this book and that magazine, then your marriage will be successful. Nonsense! I tell you that a marriage is held together by Christ. Christ must be in the midst of it. He will hold it together.

> You cannot have a successful relationship without the third party of Jesus Christ.

In all my years as a pastor, I have seen this truth so many times: People who rely on their own human love will eventually fail in their relationships. Human love can turn into hate without the love of Christ.

People who rely on human love use all the right words in the love language: "Honey pie, sweetie pie, mango pie..." They say, "I can't live life without you." Then, fast forward just two years and you will hear one saying to the other, "I don't know why I fell in love with you! I can't even stand being with you any more!" Why? Because they relied only on human love. How tragic!

If You Are Not Happy With Your Husband, Don't Go To Him, Go To Jesus

You cannot have a successful relationship without the third party of Jesus Christ. My friend, you may feel that you married the wrong person, that it's all too late and that the mistakes of the past cannot be rectified. If you feel that you are not happy with your husband, don't go to him, go to Jesus. When you're not happy with your wife, don't go to her, go to Jesus.

Too often, we go straight to the person we have a problem with to try to resolve things. And we end up angrier with that person. Instead, go to Jesus first. Spend time in His presence. Talk to Him about your marriage. Talk to Him about what is going on in your relationship. Expect Him to talk to you and believe what He says to you when He talks to you.

With Christ in the centre, you will find that

the husband draws strength from Christ, the wife draws strength from Christ and they both begin to rely less on drawing strength from one another. In marriage, it's a tragedy when what the wife is supposed to draw from the Lord, she draws instead from her husband, and her husband cannot give her what she needs because we husbands make lousy gods. Our wives may sometimes offer us burnt offerings at meal times, but we husbands still make lousy gods!

It's the same with husbands who demand from their wives things that can only come from Jesus. The husband expects her to understand his fears and insecurities. But he is meant to cast these to the Lord, to talk to the Lord about them. When he tries to cast them onto his wife, she may not understand and she may become angry. But Christ understands because He knows us best. And when Christ is in you, He holds you together. Your personality is integrated with His. This makes for a wonderful life — a life worth living!

Marriage Is Not Just About Husbands Loving Their Wives And *Vice Versa*

You know, marriage is not just about husbands loving their wives and wives loving their husbands. You might say, "But Pastor Prince, Ephesians 5:25 says, 'Husbands, love you wives.'" But it doesn't stop there! It says, *"Husbands, love your wives, just as Christ also loved the church and gave Himself for her."* Therefore, husbands are supposed to focus on how Jesus loves them because the more husbands know how much Jesus loves them, the more they will be filled with love themselves. Then, the wives will receive the overflow and the benefits of that love.

Husband, love your wife as Christ loved the church. Ephesians 5:22 says, *"Wives, submit to your own husbands, as to the Lord."* Put Jesus in your marriage, and you and your spouse will have the grace to fulfil these roles.

I tell you this, some young people are really dumb. I've met young ladies who don't want their boyfriends attending church youth meetings because they are afraid that other young ladies might snatch their boyfriends away. Don't let that kind of thinking rob you of blessings gained from attending church. When your boyfriend or husband comes to church and listens to anointed teaching, the more full of Jesus he becomes. The fuller he gets, the more he wants to share and the more he wants to spill over God's love into your life. That's the manner of God's love. When you're so full of Christ's love, you want to share it. Your partner is usually the first beneficiary.

The problem in relationships and marriages where both partners are not filled with Christ's love and don't have Christ in the centre is that we find two empty vessels trying to give and receive from each other. And we know that two empty vessels clashing against each other make a very loud noise. Husbands and wives, you need to be filled with Jesus to experience successful marriages. You might say, "Well, Pastor Prince, I don't spend time with Jesus, but I can still flow in God's grace!" Yes, grace will still be there and mercy will still be there, but you won't be able to manifest the fullness of Christ in you. To do that, you'll need to spend time with Him.

Jesus' Victory Ensures Our Victory

chapter 4

Jesus' Victory Ensures Our Victory

Victory In Life Because Of Jesus' Victory Over Death

Jesus' sacrifice on the cross was ordained by God. His death was no accident. He came for this purpose, that through death He might destroy him who had the power of death, that is, the devil. The devil had power, but Jesus destroyed his power so that He could deliver all those who through fear of death were all their lifetime subject to bondage. (Hebrews 2:14–15) That's why Jesus died — to set you free from the fear of death. Death holds no more fear for a believer.

When a non-believer dies, he wakes up more dead because he is in hell. When a Christian dies, he leaves his body, and all the pain and defects associated with a physical body. As a result, he feels that he is even more alive. And he says, "My goodness, you call this death? I feel more alive now than I was when I was in my body!" You see, your physical body restricts you.

So don't fear death. Jesus, through His death and resurrection, has conquered death for you and given you life everlasting.

Romans 6:4–5 also tells us:

> 4Therefore we were buried with Him through baptism into death, that just as Christ was raised from the dead by the glory of the Father, even so we also should walk in newness of life. 5For if we have been united together in the likeness of His death, certainly we also shall be in the likeness of His resurrection,

Church, just as we died with Christ, we are raised with Christ. His resurrection has removed the sting of death. But do you know that Jesus was also raised for your justification? (Romans 4:25) For if Christ was not raised from the dead, then you don't have forgiveness of sins. The Apostle Paul says in 1 Corinthians 15:17, *"And if Christ is not risen, your faith is futile; you are still in your sins!"* But the fact that He was raised to life means that you **have** forgiveness of all sins. (Colossians 2:13)

There are many Christians who are not living in victory today because they don't know that Jesus' resurrection not only removed the sting of death, but it also justified them. So they are still sin-conscious and afraid to draw near to God. The more we realise that we are forgiven and that there is no condemnation should we sin, the more we will have the strength to *"go and sin no more"* (John 8:11), the more we will have boldness to draw near to God and live in victory! Hebrews 10:19–22 reminds us:

> [19]**Therefore, brethren, having boldness to enter the Holiest by the blood of Jesus,** [20]**by**

a new and living way which He consecrated for us, through the veil, that is, His flesh, [21]and having a High Priest over the house of God, [22]let us draw near with a true heart in full assurance of faith, having our hearts sprinkled from an evil conscience and our bodies washed with pure water.

A New And Living Way

In the old covenant, under law, people could not draw near to God because they were sinners and God is perfect. In Exodus 19:21–22, God said to Moses on Mount Sinai:

[21]... "Go down and warn the people, lest they break through to gaze at the Lord, and many of them perish. [22]Also let the priests who come near the Lord consecrate themselves, lest the Lord break out against them."

Here, we see that the people could not come near and worship God. Why? Because they were sinners and God is holy. God is perfect and they were imperfect. In other words, God was telling them, "Don't come near Me or My glory will destroy you." So under law, the more they came to God, the higher their chances of perishing!

However, today, we are no longer under law. The new covenant reveals to us that we are under grace. The blood of Jesus covers us and our sins have been forgiven. Hebrews 10:19–20 says:

> [19]Therefore, brethren, having boldness to enter the Holiest by the blood of Jesus, [20]by a new and living way which He consecrated for us…

So we see that under grace, we can have boldness to come into God's presence by the blood of Jesus — and we will not perish! In fact, it is *a new and living way*!

Worshipping Jesus Brings Wholeness

The more we come into God's presence, having been consecrated by the blood of Jesus

(Hebrews 10:20), the more we live. Thank God we now live under grace! Hebrews 10:20 calls it *"a new and living way"*. Why is it called a "living way"? Doesn't God know that everyone whose heart is beating is alive and living? Of course He knows, but a "living way" here means that the more you come to God, the more every part of you — spirit, soul and body — will live.

The Bible says that under law, those with marks or defects — those who were crippled, hunch-backed and diseased — could not come near and worship God. But under grace, all those with marks or defects could come to Jesus. They worshipped Him and He made them well, He made them whole. Under grace, they found a new and living way!

I love the passages in the gospels (Matthew 15:30–31, Luke 4:40) where it says that the multitude brought all those who were lame, blind, dumb and maimed ("maimed" implies missing body parts!) to Jesus. I can just see them queuing up to seek healing from Jesus and being made whole! We all have physical defects or imperfections, and the more we worship Him and the more we come to Him, the more He makes us whole and the more we live.

You know, worship is a privilege. When the worship leader in your church says, "Lift your hands!" you are not doing it for his benefit, you are doing it for your own benefit. Every time you lift your hands to worship the Lord, every time you draw near to Him, an imperfection in you is being corrected, and you are being adjusted and made whole. That is a new and living way!

How Does Jesus Speak To Us?

So the more you draw close to God today, the more He makes you whole in every way. God wants you to come to Him and commune with Him. In fact, the Bible says in John 7:37, *"If anyone thirsts, let him come to Me and drink."* What does Jesus mean? He means that He wants to satisfy our thirst for His presence, for His closeness, for His intimacy, for His loving words.

Many people try to hear from Jesus by expecting Him to speak to them through another person as He did in the old covenant. Some

Christians still run to prophets to hear God's word for them. Or they run to conferences for prophetic words. In the old covenant, people heard God speak to them through prophets. They heard God speak to them through a third party.

Today, there is no need for prophets to direct us. They tell us things to confirm what God has already placed in our hearts. That's because in the new covenant, God says, *"None of them shall teach his neighbour, and none his brother, saying, 'Know the Lord,' for all shall know Me, from the least of them to the greatest of them."* (Hebrews 8:11) You will see that this is true in the book of Acts. When the Holy Spirit spoke through the prophets and teachers there to separate Paul and Barnabas for the work He had called them to, it was no surprise to them. (Acts 13:1–3) It was just a confirmation.

Many today also expect God to speak to them directly in an audible voice. In the old covenant, that was how God spoke to the prophets. And that's why some Christians still expect God to speak to them in a deep booming voice like in the movie, *The Ten Commandments*.

Only very rarely does He speak to us audibly today.

Under the new covenant, we hear God's voice from within. We no longer rely on God to speak to us through a third person or in a clear, audible voice. Today, God tends to speak to us from inside us. If God wants you to call someone, He won't say, "Call So-and-so!" Why? Because you and God are one. 1 Corinthians 6:17 says, *"But he who is joined to the Lord is one spirit with Him."*

> Christ speaks to us, in us and through us because we are one spirit with Him.

Because we are *"one spirit with Him"*, God now speaks to us through the Holy Spirit who is within us. So when you will feel like calling So-and-so, do it straightaway. You don't have to ask, "Is this God?" You just go ahead and be led by that desire. Today, God very rarely speaks audibly to us. Instead, He leads us by an inner "knowing", an inner desire or a still, small voice in our hearts.

God Is Leading Us All The Time, Every Day

Christ speaks **to** us, **in** us and **through** us because we are one spirit with Him. We are therefore tied to Him in one spirit and with one voice. And God does not normally speak to us in a spectacular fashion, nonetheless, His voice is supernatural. And we who are sensitive to His Spirit will hear His voice.

When you practise hearing the Father, often, you'll hear Him speak to you with loving words like, "Well done, son! I'm glad you gave that up for me," or "I'm glad you're doing that, son!" That's how He speaks to us most of the time. He won't tell you, "Go down this alley, buy four numbers that I shall give thee and surely you shall strike the first prize. It shall be the biggest lottery win in history, and it shall set you and your family free in the Year of Jubilee. So it shall be, for I have spoken unto thee." Some Christians expect Jesus to speak to them like that! They run to prophetic conferences to try and find Jesus speaking like that.

God is leading us all the time, every day. Most times, He doesn't speak to us in big spectacular ways. He just says to us, "Son, I love you. Come, walk by the beach with Me. Come, walk down here with Me. Just stay a bit longer down here and just talk to Me." That's how He speaks to you. That's how He loves you.

'If Anyone Thirsts, Let Him Come To Me And Drink'

God wants a close relationship with you more than you know. That's why He says in John 7:37, *"If anyone thirsts, let him come to Me and drink."* He wants to fulfil His promise to meet our deep need for intimacy. He tells us to just drink and drink and drink His presence. And what's the result? The next line says, *"He who believes in Me, as the Scripture has said, out of his heart will flow rivers of living water."* (John 7:38)

You know, the rivers of living water are for the benefit of the people around you. The rivers are for **them** to drink from as well. When I come to Jesus and I satisfy my thirst, all of a sudden, rivers start flowing out of me. I become a blessing to others around me. If I didn't drink from Him,

I would have no overflow for others to drink from.

In John 4, we find that the disciples went away to the city to buy Jesus lunch. A Samaritan woman came to draw water and she met Jesus sitting at Jacob's well. John 4:6 tells us, *"Now Jacob's well was there. Jesus therefore, being wearied from His journey, sat thus by the well."* They began talking and after He spoke revelations to the Samaritan woman and revealed Himself to her as the Messiah, Jesus was refreshed. He was so refreshed that when His disciples returned, they thought someone had given Him food for He said to them, *"I have food to eat of which you do not know."* (John 4:32) God delights in us drawing from Him. It refreshes Him. It's food for Him!

He loves being around you. Matthew 18:20 tells us, *"For where two or three are gathered together in My name, I am there in the midst of*

> He knows what makes a great marriage because He came up with the concept of marriage.

them." Husband and wife, when you wake up each morning, acknowledge Jesus' presence. He's in your midst. He doesn't wait for you to come to church to say, "Hello, Jesus!" He is with you when you wake up in the morning. Aren't you glad of this promise? The Lord is so gracious to us. Although He is high and mighty, He doesn't ask for a big group. He breaks it down to the lowest plurality — two or three!

Jesus Knows What Makes A Great Marriage

Whether you're married or you're dating, Jesus is there in your midst. For the good of your marriage and for the good of your relationship, acknowledge Him and talk to Him. And expect Him to speak to you because He will. He'll tell you things like, "Just go and kiss your wife right now!" You may say, "That's not Jesus. Jesus is not that romantic!" But He is! He is the creator of romance! He knows what makes a great marriage because He came up with the concept of marriage. And He promises that He will be in the midst of us. His place is always in the centre.

Today, Jesus is unlimited. After He rose again, He became both physical and spiritual. This means that He can appear and disappear. In John 20:19, when He appeared to His disciples, where did He appear? Jesus came and stood in the **midst** of them. And He said to them, *"Peace be with you."*

Verse 20 goes on to say:

> ²⁰**When He had said this, He showed them His hands and His side. Then the disciples were glad when they saw the Lord.**

You see, peace can only come when you know the finished work of Christ. When the disciples saw Jesus, His hands and His side, they were glad. Like the disciples, we too, gain gladness and peace when we see the Lord and His finished work. My friend, do you see Jesus and His finished work in you? Are you placing Him in the centre of your career, your marriage, your business?

John shows us in Revelation 5:5–6 that Jesus, the Lion of the tribe of Judah, has prevailed:

> ⁵**But one of the elders said to me, "Do not**

weep. Behold, the Lion of the tribe of Judah, the Root of David, has prevailed to open the scroll and to loose its seven seals." [6]And I looked, and behold, in the midst of the throne and of the four living creatures, and in the midst of the elders, stood a Lamb as though it had been slain, having seven horns and seven eyes, which are the seven Spirits of God sent out into all the earth.

It is important to note that seven is the number of perfection in the Bible. So when we see that the Lamb has seven horns and seven eyes, it symbolises perfect authority and perfect discernment. Jesus is both Lion and Lamb, God and Man, majesty and meekness!

Verses 11–13 continue:

[11]Then I looked, and I heard the voice of many angels around the throne, the living creatures, and the elders; and the number of them was ten thousand times ten thousand, and thousands of thousands, [12]saying with a loud voice: "Worthy is the Lamb who was slain to receive power and riches and

wisdom, and strength and honour and glory and blessing!"

¹³And every creature which is in heaven and on the earth and under the earth and such as are in the sea, and all that are in them, I heard saying: "Blessing and honour and glory and power be to Him who sits on the throne, and to the Lamb, forever and ever!"

Here, we see that though Jesus is high and lifted up, He is also humble. Revelation 1:13 (KJV) shows us how humble He is. John says that he saw Jesus wearing *"a golden girdle"*. Now, a girdle is a servant's towel. A servant uses a girdle to serve. Even when Jesus was on earth, He washed His disciples' feet. (John 13:3–12) Even though Jesus has *"power and riches and wisdom and strength and honour and glory and blessing"* (Revelation 5:12), He still wants to serve us! Why? Because He loves us so much.

That's why Jesus deserves to be the centrepiece of our lives. And when He does, we become held together, integrated with Him, full of His love and rich towards Him. When He is the centrepiece of our lives, we are constantly conscious of His presence in our lives, we have a close relationship with Him, we are led by Him, and we find meaning and purpose in life. That, brothers and sisters, is truly a life worth living!

Start Living Now

Friend, do you want to start living the abundant life that Jesus meant for you to live? You may say, "Yes, but how do I start?" God wants you to understand that the law of the old covenant makes you conscious of self — of past regrets, of your failures, of your inabilities. But the grace of the new covenant makes you conscious of Christ. And when you become conscious of Jesus, conscious of His love for you, conscious of all that He has done for you at the cross, placing Him in the centre of your life is the only thing you'll want to do. So start looking to Jesus. Start focusing on His beauty and start enjoying His love. That's how you live a life worth living!

Now, go and live it! And you will experience His thousand-fold blessing!

Salvation Prayer

If you would like to receive all that Jesus has done for you, and make Him your Lord and Saviour, please pray this prayer:

Lord Jesus, thank You for loving me and dying for me on the cross. Your precious blood washes me clean of every sin. You are my Lord and my Savior, now and forever. I believe that You rose from the dead and that You are alive today. Because of Your finished work, I am now a beloved child of God and heaven is my home. Thank You for giving me eternal life, and filling my heart with Your peace and joy. Amen.

We Would Like To Hear From You

If you have prayed the salvation prayer, or if you have a testimony to share after reading this book, please send it to us via JosephPrince.com/testimony.

Other Materials By Joseph Prince

We trust that you have been blessed reading this book. For the latest, most exclusive and best-priced Joseph Prince resources, visit www.JosephPrince.com.